CHRIS KREIDER BIOGRAPHY

Heart of the Rangers: Making History on Madison Square Garden Ice

AMBER SPENCER

CHRIS KREIDER BIOGRAPHY

Copyright ©AMBER SPENCER, 2024. All rights reserved. No part of this publication may be
reproduced, distributed, or transmitted in any form or by any means, including photocopying, recording, or other electronic or mechanical methods, without the prior written permission of the publisher, except in the case of brief quotations embodied in critical reviews and certain other noncommercial uses permitted by copyright law.

CHRIS KREIDER BIOGRAPHY

DISCLAIMER

This book contains information that is solely meant to be educational. Despite their best efforts to present accurate and current information, the author and publisher disclaim all expressed and implied representations and warranties regarding the availability, completeness, accuracy, reliability, suitability, or suitability of the content contained herein for any purpose. The publisher and the author disclaim all responsibility for any loss or harm, including without limitation, consequential or indirect loss or damage, or any loss or damage at all resulting from lost profits or data resulting from using this book.

CHRIS KREIDER BIOGRAPHY

TABLE OF CONTENT

INTRODUCTION: THE MAKING OF A RANGER

CHAPTER 1: ROOTS IN BOXFORD (1991-2004)

CHAPTER 2: THE PHILLIPS ACADEMY YEARS (2004-2009)

CHAPTER 3: BOSTON COLLEGE GOLDEN ERA (2009-2012)

CHAPTER 4: THE RANGERS DEBUT (2012)

CHAPTER 5: THE RANGERS DEBUT (2012)

CHAPTER 6: GROWING YEARS (2012-2017)

CHAPTER 7: LEADERSHIP EVOLUTION (2017-2020)

CHAPTER 8: RECORD-BREAKING SEASONS (2021-2024)

CHAPTER 9: THE HEART OF BROADWAY

CHAPTER 10: PERSONAL LIFE AND VALUES

CHAPTER 11: PLAYING STYLE ANALYSIS

EPILOGUE

CHRIS KREIDER BIOGRAPHY

INTRODUCTION: THE MAKING OF A RANGER

Chris Kreider's story is more than just another hockey tale – it's a journey that perfectly captures the American dream in sports. Born on April 30, 1991, in Boxford, Massachusetts, Kreider's path to becoming one of the New York Rangers' most important players shows what happens when natural talent meets endless dedication.

From his early days playing hockey in Massachusetts, Kreider stood out for his unusual combination of size and speed. Even as a young player, he caught everyone's attention with his ability to move faster than smaller players despite his growing frame. This rare mix of physical gifts would later become his trademark in the NHL, but the path to professional success wasn't always clear or easy.

The story of Kreider's rise in hockey is special because he didn't follow the usual route many NHL stars take. Instead of joining junior hockey leagues, he chose to develop his skills through prep school and college hockey. His time at Phillips Academy Andover showed his commitment to both education and athletics – a balance that would shape his approach to professional hockey later on. During these formative years, he wasn't just a hockey player; he was also a talented soccer player and track athlete, building the diverse athletic skills that would later serve him well on the ice.

CHRIS KREIDER BIOGRAPHY

His decision to attend Boston College, one of the most respected college hockey programs in the United States, proved to be a turning point. Under the guidance of legendary coach Jerry York, Kreider's game evolved from raw talent to refined skill. During his three years at BC (2009-2012), he helped lead the Eagles to two NCAA championships, showing he could perform at his best in the biggest moments. His college years weren't just about hockey success – they were about growing as a person and learning how to handle pressure and expectations.

The New York Rangers saw something special in Kreider before anyone else, selecting him 19th overall in the 2009 NHL Entry Draft. This choice would prove to be one of the most important draft decisions in recent Rangers history. What makes Kreider's story particularly interesting is how he made his NHL debut – jumping straight from winning a national championship with Boston College into the 2012 NHL playoffs. Most players need time to adjust to professional hockey, but Kreider scored his first NHL goal in the playoffs, showing right away that he belonged at the highest level.

The years that followed showed Kreider's dedication to improving every aspect of his game. He worked through the typical challenges young players face – learning to be consistent, dealing with injuries, and handling the pressure of playing in New York City, one of hockey's biggest markets. What stands out about Kreider is how he kept getting better year after year, when many players plateau early in their careers.

CHRIS KREIDER BIOGRAPHY

His breakthrough 2021-22 season, where he scored 52 goals, wasn't just a personal triumph – it was a reward for years of steady improvement and hard work. This achievement made him the fourth player in Rangers history to score 50 goals in a season, putting him in the company of legends like Vic Hadfield, Adam Graves, and Jaromir Jagr. It wasn't just about scoring goals; Kreider had become a complete player who could help his team in many ways – killing penalties, providing leadership, and being a positive influence in the community.

Off the ice, Kreider breaks the stereotype of the typical hockey player. He's known for his intelligence and ability to speak multiple languages, including Russian and Spanish. He uses these skills to help younger teammates, especially those coming from other countries,

CHRIS KREIDER BIOGRAPHY

feel welcome and adjust to life in New York. His involvement in team leadership and community work shows how much he cares about more than just his personal success.

The relationship between Kreider and Madison Square Garden, the Rangers' home arena known as "The World's Most Famous Arena," has become special. In a city known for being tough on athletes, Kreider has earned the respect and love of New York fans through his consistent effort and clutch performances. His style of play – fast, physical, and fearless – matches perfectly with what Rangers fans expect from their players.

Looking at Kreider's career so far, what stands out most is his steady growth from a promising rookie to one of the Rangers' most reliable leaders. He's become known for his net-front presence on power plays, his incredible speed on breakaways, and his ability to come through in big moments. His journey from Massachusetts to Madison Square Garden shows that the path to NHL success doesn't always follow the expected route.

Today, Kreider represents the heart of the Rangers organization. His career is a blueprint for young players, showing how combining natural talent with hard work, education, and dedication can lead to lasting success in professional sports. As he continues to add to his legacy with the Rangers, his story remains an inspiring example of how to build a meaningful career in professional hockey while making a positive impact both on and off the ice.

CHAPTER 1: ROOTS IN BOXFORD (1991-2004)

The story of Chris Kreider's early years begins in the small, historic town of Boxford, Massachusetts, where he was born on April 30, 1991. Boxford, with its population of just over 8,000 people, provided the perfect backdrop for a young athlete to develop his talents. The town, located in Essex County, was known for its strong community values and emphasis on youth sports, creating an environment where young Chris could thrive.

David and Kathy Kreider, Chris's parents, played crucial roles in shaping his early life and athletic development. David, working in construction management, taught Chris the value of hard work and attention to detail from an early age. Kathy, a middle school physical education teacher, naturally influenced his athletic pursuits and understanding of physical fitness. Their support and guidance would prove invaluable throughout his journey.

The Kreider household was always active, with sports being a central part of daily life. Chris grew up with his sister, Katie, who also shared the family's athletic inclinations. The siblings often engaged in friendly competition, pushing each other to improve in various sports and activities. This sibling rivalry helped build Chris's competitive spirit from an early age.

Winter in Boxford meant one thing for young Chris - hockey season. The cold Massachusetts winters provided plenty of opportunities for outdoor skating, and Chris took full advantage of this. Local ponds would freeze over, becoming natural rinks where neighborhood kids gathered to play pickup games. These informal sessions on pond ice helped develop the kind of creativity and adaptability that would later become hallmarks of Kreider's playing style.

His first organized hockey experience came at the age of six when he joined the Boxford Youth Hockey Association. Even in these earliest days of organized play, coaches noticed something different about young Chris. While most children his age were still learning to skate properly, Kreider showed unusual balance and coordination. His natural athletic ability was evident, but what stood out most was his eagerness to learn and improve.

CHRIS KREIDER BIOGRAPHY

The local youth hockey program exposed Chris to structured training for the first time. Here, he learned the fundamental skills that would form the foundation of his future career - skating techniques, puck handling, and basic hockey strategy. His coaches from these early years remember him as an attentive student of the game, always asking questions and seeking to understand the 'why' behind every drill and technique.

During his elementary school years at Harry Lee Cole Elementary School, Chris's athletic abilities extended far beyond the hockey rink. He participated in several sports, including soccer, baseball, and track. This multi-sport approach in his early years would prove beneficial, helping him develop different muscle groups and various athletic skills that would later complement his hockey abilities.

The Kreider family home became a hub of athletic activity. Their driveway hosted countless street hockey games, and the basement was transformed into a practice area where Chris could work on his stick handling skills. His father installed a net in the basement, allowing Chris to practice his shooting even during the off-season. This dedication to practice, even at a young age, set the foundation for his future work ethic.

Financial sacrifices were a reality for the Kreider family, as youth hockey equipment and travel team expenses added up quickly. His parents worked extra hours to ensure Chris could participate in the best available programs. This sacrifice wasn't lost on young Chris, who showed his gratitude through his commitment to improvement and his responsible approach to both sports and academics.

The local community played a significant role in Chris's development. Boxford's tight-knit nature meant that neighbors, teachers, and coaches all contributed to his growth. Many residents remember him as the kid who was always carrying a hockey stick, whether walking to school or playing with friends. The community's support system helped create an environment where his talents could flourish.

Around age 10, Chris began playing for the Valley Junior Warriors, a more competitive youth hockey program in the region. This step up in competition level exposed him to better

CHRIS KREIDER BIOGRAPHY

players and more structured coaching. It was during this time that his exceptional skating speed began to emerge as a distinctive trait. Despite being one of the larger kids on his team, he could outskate many of his smaller, theoretically more agile teammates.

The Warriors' program introduced Chris to more serious training regimens and travel hockey. Weekend tournaments became regular events, taking the Kreider family across New England. These tournaments provided valuable experience in playing different styles of hockey and competing against varied levels of competition. It was also during this time that Chris began to understand the importance of teamwork and leadership.

CHRIS KREIDER BIOGRAPHY

Academic excellence was always emphasized in the Kreider household, alongside athletic achievement. At Boxford's Spofford Pond Elementary School, Chris proved to be as dedicated to his studies as he was to sports. His teachers from this period remember him as a bright, engaged student who managed to balance his increasing athletic commitments with his schoolwork - a skill that would serve him well in his later academic and athletic career.

The influence of professional hockey, particularly the Boston Bruins, played a significant role in Chris's childhood. Growing up in Massachusetts meant exposure to one of the NHL's Original Six teams, and Chris attended several Bruins games at the FleetCenter (now TD Garden). These experiences helped shape his understanding of professional hockey and fueled his dreams of playing at the highest level.

By the age of 12, Chris was already showing signs of the physical attributes that would later define his NHL career. He was taller than most of his peers and possessed unusual coordination for his size. Youth coaches began to recognize that they had someone special on their hands, though few could have predicted just how far his talents would take him.

The family's approach to Chris's development wasn't just focused on hockey skills. His mother's background in physical education meant that proper nutrition and overall fitness were emphasized from an early age. This holistic approach to athletic development helped prevent early specialization and burnout, issues that often plague young athletes.

Baseball provided a welcome counterbalance to hockey during the spring and summer months. Playing as a pitcher and outfielder, Chris developed different athletic skills that would later translate to hockey in unexpected ways. The hand-eye coordination required for batting and the explosive movements needed for pitching contributed to his overall athletic development.

The local library became another important venue in young Chris's life. His parents encouraged reading and learning alongside his athletic pursuits, helping him develop into a well-rounded individual. This intellectual curiosity, fostered during his early years in

Boxford, would later surprise many who encountered him in the professional hockey world.

As he approached his teenage years, his size and speed combination began to draw attention from prep school scouts. His parents, particularly his father, began researching the best path forward for their son's development. They understood that the next few years would be crucial in determining Chris's athletic future.

The Boxford community continued to play a supportive role as Chris's talents became more apparent. Local businesses sponsored his teams, and community members often helped with transportation to games and tournaments. This community support system demonstrated the

CHRIS KREIDER BIOGRAPHY

small-town values that would influence Chris's character throughout his career.

Youth coaches remember Chris's unusual ability to process and apply instruction. While many young players needed multiple repetitions to grasp new concepts, he often understood and implemented new techniques quickly. This mental aptitude for the game, combined with his physical gifts, suggested that he had the potential for a special career in hockey.

The end of his time in Boxford youth hockey coincided with important decisions about his future development. As he prepared to enter his teenage years, it became clear that Chris would need to seek out more challenging competition to continue his development. His years in Boxford had provided him with a strong

CHRIS KREIDER BIOGRAPHY

foundation - not just in hockey skills, but in character, work ethic, and values.

Looking back on these formative years in Boxford, it's clear that the combination of family support, community involvement, and natural ability set Chris Kreider on a path to success. The small town values, emphasis on education, and exposure to multiple sports all contributed to developing the person who would later become a star for the New York Rangers.

These early years in Boxford weren't just about learning hockey - they were about building character, developing work ethic, and understanding the importance of community. The lessons learned during this period would prove invaluable as Chris moved forward in his

CHRIS KREIDER BIOGRAPHY

hockey career, facing bigger challenges and higher levels of competition.

The town of Boxford continues to take pride in Chris Kreider's achievements, seeing him as a hometown success story. His journey from the local ponds and rinks to the NHL serves as inspiration for young athletes in the community, showing that with talent, dedication, and support, dreams of playing professional sports can become reality.

CHRIS KREIDER BIOGRAPHY

CHAPTER 2: THE PHILLIPS ACADEMY YEARS (2004-2009)

Chris Kreider's arrival at Phillips Academy Andover in 2004 marked the beginning of a crucial phase in his development, both as an athlete and as a student. Phillips Academy, one of America's oldest and most prestigious boarding schools, would provide the structured environment where Kreider's raw talent could be refined and his academic abilities could flourish.

The decision to attend Phillips Academy wasn't made lightly by the Kreider family. The school, founded in 1778, was known for its rigorous academic standards and its tradition of

CHRIS KREIDER BIOGRAPHY

excellence in athletics. Located just a short distance from Boxford in Andover, Massachusetts, the school offered Chris the opportunity to continue his development while remaining close to his family support system.

Adjusting to life at Phillips Academy presented new challenges. The academic demands were significantly higher than what Chris had experienced before, with long days of classes followed by athletic commitments. The school's motto, "Non Sibi" (Not for Self), aligned well with the values Chris had learned in Boxford, emphasizing the importance of contributing to the larger community.

During his freshman year, Kreider's unusual athletic abilities quickly caught the attention of the school's coaching staff. While most freshmen

CHRIS KREIDER BIOGRAPHY

struggled to make varsity teams, Chris earned spots on multiple varsity squads. His physical development was accelerating, and he was already showing signs of the impressive speed-size combination that would later define his professional career.

The hockey program at Phillips Academy, under the guidance of head coach Dean Boylan, provided structured development opportunities that hadn't been available in youth hockey. Boylan, an experienced coach with a track record of developing college-level players, recognized Kreider's potential and began working to refine his raw talents.

Academic life at Phillips required significant adjustment. The school's demanding curriculum included required courses in English, mathematics, science, history, and foreign languages. Chris chose to study Spanish, displaying an aptitude for languages that would later become useful in his professional career. His teachers noted his strong work ethic, which matched his dedication to athletics.

Phillips Academy's athletic facilities provided Kreider with resources he hadn't previously had access to. The school's ice rink, weight room, and training facilities were available year-round, allowing him to maintain his development even during the off-season. The school's strength and conditioning program helped him build the physical foundation that would serve him well in his future career.

Soccer became an important part of Kreider's athletic development at Phillips. Playing as a striker, he used his speed and size to dominate opponents on the soccer field. The cardiovascular conditioning and footwork skills developed through soccer complemented his hockey training, contributing to his exceptional skating ability.

Track and field provided another outlet for Kreider's athletic talents. His performances in sprinting events were particularly notable, as he consistently posted times that were unusual for someone of his size. The explosion and acceleration developed through track training would later translate directly to his skating stride on the ice.

The hockey season remained the primary focus of Kreider's athletic pursuits. Phillips Academy competed in the highly regarded New England

CHRIS KREIDER BIOGRAPHY

Prep School Ice Hockey Association, facing some of the best high school teams in the region. During his sophomore year, Chris began to emerge as one of the league's standout players, drawing attention from college scouts.

Living on campus exposed Chris to a diverse community of students from around the world. This experience broadened his perspectives and helped develop his social skills. His roommates and classmates remember him as someone who balanced his intense athletic focus with a genuine interest in others and a good sense of humor.

The school's tradition of "total student development" meant that Chris had to participate in activities beyond sports and academics. He became involved in community service projects, working with local youth hockey programs and participating in school outreach initiatives. These experiences helped develop his leadership skills and sense of social responsibility.

By his junior year, Kreider's hockey abilities were drawing significant attention from college recruiters and professional scouts. His combination of size, speed, and skill was unusual for a high school player. Despite the increasing attention, he maintained his focus on both academic and athletic development at Phillips.

The school's college counseling program helped Chris navigate the complex process of college recruitment while maintaining his amateur status. This was particularly important as his draft prospects began to rise, and professional teams showed interest in his development.

Academic success continued alongside athletic achievements. Kreider maintained strong grades despite his demanding athletic schedule, impressing teachers with his ability to manage his time effectively. His performance in advanced placement courses demonstrated intellectual capabilities that went beyond his athletic talents.

Leadership roles began to come naturally to Kreider during his upper years at Phillips. He served as a prefect in his dormitory, helping younger students adjust to boarding school life. On athletic teams, he led by example, setting high standards for work ethic and preparation.

CHRIS KREIDER BIOGRAPHY

The school's winter term was particularly intense, with hockey season in full swing alongside challenging academic requirements. Kreider developed effective time management skills, often studying late into the night after practices and games. This discipline would prove valuable in his college years and beyond.

Relations with teammates at Phillips were strengthened by the boarding school environment, where students lived together and shared daily experiences. Many of these friendships would continue throughout his career, providing a support network outside of hockey.

During his senior year, Kreider's development culminated in several school records for hockey performance. His scoring totals and physical play drew comparisons to previous Phillips Academy athletes who had gone on to successful college and professional careers.

The college recruitment process intensified during his final year, with multiple Division I programs expressing interest. Boston College emerged as a leading candidate, offering both strong academics and one of the nation's top hockey programs. The decision would need to balance his athletic development with his academic goals.

Preparation for the NHL draft became another consideration during his senior year. Scouts were regular attendees at Phillips Academy games, evaluating Kreider's potential as a professional prospect. The school's staff helped him manage

CHRIS KREIDER BIOGRAPHY

these additional pressures while maintaining focus on his immediate responsibilities.

As graduation approached, Kreider had developed into more than just an exceptional athlete. Phillips Academy had helped shape him into a well-rounded individual with strong academic capabilities and leadership skills. His transformation from a talented youth player to a college-ready student-athlete was complete.

The impact of his Phillips Academy years would continue to influence Kreider's approach to both hockey and life. The school's emphasis on excellence in all areas, commitment to service, and high academic standards helped form the character traits that would serve him well in his future career.

CHRIS KREIDER BIOGRAPHY

Looking back, the Phillips Academy period represented a crucial transition in Kreider's development. The combination of elite academic instruction, high-level athletic competition, and character development created the foundation for his future success in college hockey and eventually the NHL.

Kreider's time at Phillips Academy concluded with both athletic honors and academic achievements. He graduated in 2009, ready to face the challenges of Division I college hockey and higher education. The skills, values, and experiences gained during these formative years would prove invaluable in the next phase of his journey.

The legacy of Kreider's years at Phillips Academy extends beyond his individual achievements. His success story serves as an inspiration to current students, demonstrating how the school's combination of academic rigor and athletic excellence can prepare students for success at the highest levels of sport and education.

Today, Phillips Academy continues to recognize Kreider's achievements, featuring his story as an example of how the school's mission to educate "youth from every quarter" can help develop well-rounded individuals capable of success in multiple areas of life. His years at the school represent a model of how athletic talent can be developed alongside academic excellence and character formation.

CHAPTER 3: BOSTON COLLEGE GOLDEN ERA (2009-2012)

Chris Kreider's arrival at Boston College in the fall of 2009 marked the beginning of what would become one of the most successful periods in the school's storied hockey program. Located in Chestnut Hill, Massachusetts, Boston College offered the perfect blend of elite academics and championship-caliber hockey that Kreider sought for his collegiate career.

The transition from Phillips Academy to Division I college hockey presented new challenges. The speed and physicality of the college game were significantly different from prep school hockey. However, Kreider's unusual combination of size and speed, developed during his years at Phillips, allowed him to adapt quickly to the elevated level of play.

Under the guidance of legendary coach Jerry York, Kreider's freshman year began with intensive training sessions designed to refine his raw talents. York, known for his ability to develop NHL-caliber players, recognized the unique attributes Kreider possessed. The veteran coach implemented specific drills and training regimens to enhance Kreider's already impressive skating abilities and shooting skills.

Living in the Walsh Hall dormitory during his freshman year, Kreider quickly became part of the tight-knit Boston College community. His roommates remember him as someone who maintained a strict routine, balancing early morning workouts with late-night study sessions. This discipline helped him manage the demands of being a student-athlete at one of the nation's top academic institutions.

The Carroll School of Management at Boston College provided Kreider with challenging coursework that complemented his athletic pursuits. His choice to major in Communications reflected his interest in developing skills beyond hockey. Professors noted his engagement in class discussions and ability to meet academic deadlines despite his demanding hockey schedule.

His freshman season exceeded expectations as he contributed significantly to Boston College's success. His speed became legendary on campus, with teammates and opponents alike marveling at his ability to accelerate past defenders. The Eagles' high-tempo system perfectly suited his playing style, allowing him to showcase his unique abilities.

The 2010 NCAA Championship run during his freshman year proved to be a defining moment. Kreider played a crucial role in the Eagles' success, scoring key goals throughout the tournament. The championship victory over Wisconsin at Ford Field in Detroit provided his first taste of high-stakes hockey success, an experience that would prove valuable in his future professional career.

Practice sessions at Conte Forum became opportunities for Kreider to develop new aspects of his game. Coach York emphasized the importance of playing in all three zones, helping Chris evolve from a purely offensive player into a more complete hockey player. The coaching staff worked extensively on his positioning, defensive awareness, and special teams play.

The Hockey East conference provided strong competition throughout the season. Rivals like Boston University, Maine, and New Hampshire pushed Kreider to elevate his game. The intensity of these matchups, particularly the Beanpot Tournament games, helped prepare him for the professional level.

Academic support services at Boston College played a crucial role in Kreider's success. The school's learning resources center helped him develop study strategies that accommodated his demanding schedule. His academic advisors worked closely with the hockey program to ensure he could maintain high standards in both areas.

Team traditions at Boston College helped shape Kreider's understanding of hockey culture. The maroon and gold jersey represented more than just a uniform – it carried the legacy of Eagles hockey excellence. Pre-game rituals, team meetings, and post-game celebrations all contributed to his development as a team player.

During his sophomore year, Kreider's role on the team expanded. Coach York gave him more responsibility in key situations, including power play and penalty kill duties. His ability to use his speed effectively in all situations made him a valuable asset in multiple game scenarios.

CHRIS KREIDER BIOGRAPHY

The weight room became a second home for Kreider during his college years. Strength and conditioning coach Russell DeRosa developed specialized programs to help Chris maintain his speed while adding muscle mass. These training sessions laid the groundwork for the physical style he would later employ in the NHL.

Community service remained important during his Boston College years. The team participated in various charitable activities, including youth hockey clinics and hospital visits. These experiences helped Kreider maintain perspective and develop leadership skills that would serve him well in his professional career.

Away from the rink, Kreider explored Boston's rich history and culture. The city's professional sports environment, particularly the presence of the Bruins, provided constant reminders of his ultimate goal. He often attended NHL games at TD Garden, studying the professionals he hoped to join.

The Eagles' practice facility became a laboratory for skill development. Hours of extra practice after team sessions helped Kreider refine his shot, improve his stickhandling, and work on the finer points of his game. Teammates remember his dedication to improvement, often being the last player to leave the ice.

Junior year brought new challenges and opportunities. NHL teams were tracking his development closely, as the Rangers had drafted him in the first round. The pressure to perform increased, but Kreider maintained his focus on team success and individual improvement.

CHRIS KREIDER BIOGRAPHY

The 2012 NCAA Championship campaign during his junior year showcased Kreider's complete development as a player. His contributions went beyond scoring, as he became a leader both on and off the ice. The championship victory served as a perfect culmination of his college career.

Throughout his time at Boston College, Kreider maintained strong relationships with his prep school mentors and former coaches. This support network helped him navigate the challenges of college hockey and academic life. Their guidance proved particularly valuable as he approached decisions about his professional career.

CHRIS KREIDER BIOGRAPHY

International experience came through participation in World Junior Championships during his college years. Representing Team USA provided additional high-level competition and helped broaden his hockey perspective. These tournaments allowed him to measure himself against top players from other countries.

The Boston College alumni network, particularly former Eagles playing in the NHL, provided valuable mentorship. Their experiences helped Kreider understand the challenges ahead as he prepared for professional hockey. These connections would prove valuable during his transition to the NHL.

Academic achievements during his college years demonstrated Kreider's commitment to education. His performance in the classroom matched his efforts on the ice, earning him academic honors and respect from professors and peers alike. This balance would later influence his approach to professional development.

Team chemistry at Boston College played a crucial role in the program's success during Kreider's tenure. The bonds formed with teammates extended beyond the rink, creating lasting friendships and a support system that would continue throughout his professional career.

As his college career neared its end, Kreider had evolved into a complete player ready for professional hockey. His development at Boston College had enhanced every aspect of his game while providing him with an education and experiences that would benefit him throughout his life.

Looking back, the Boston College years represented the perfect bridge between amateur and professional hockey for Kreider. The program's emphasis on both individual skill development and team success prepared him for the challenges ahead in the NHL.

The legacy of his time at Boston College extends beyond his individual achievements. His success story became part of the program's rich history, inspiring future Eagles players to pursue excellence in both athletics and academics. His contributions to two national championships helped maintain Boston College's position among college hockey's elite programs.

CHRIS KREIDER BIOGRAPHY

Today, Chris Kreider is remembered at Boston College not just for his athletic achievements, but for his commitment to personal growth and team success. His years with the Eagles demonstrate how the right collegiate program can develop both an elite athlete and a well-rounded individual prepared for success at the highest levels of professional sports.

CHRIS KREIDER BIOGRAPHY

CHAPTER 4: THE RANGERS DEBUT (2012)

The spring of 2012 marked a pivotal moment in Chris Kreider's hockey career as he made the unprecedented jump from college hockey straight into the NHL playoffs with the New York Rangers. His transition from Boston College's national championship celebration to Madison Square Garden's playoff intensity happened in a matter of days, creating one of the most remarkable debut stories in NHL history.

On April 7, 2012, Kreider was celebrating his second NCAA championship with Boston College. Just three days later, on April 10, he signed his entry-level contract with the New York Rangers. The timing was extraordinary –

the Rangers were preparing for their first-round playoff series against the Ottawa Senators, and the team's management made the bold decision to add the untested rookie to their playoff roster.

The Rangers' training staff worked intensively with Kreider during his first days with the team, helping him adjust to the NHL's pace and systems. Head coach John Tortorella, known for his demanding style, had to balance the desire to utilize Kreider's obvious talents with the need to protect a rookie in high-stakes playoff situations.

Kreider's first NHL practice at the Rangers' training facility in Greenburgh, New York, gave his teammates their first glimpse of his exceptional speed. Veterans on the team were immediately impressed by his physical tools, though they understood the enormous challenge he faced in adapting to playoff hockey without any regular season experience.

The Madison Square Garden debut came in Game 3 of the first-round series against Ottawa. The historic arena, known as "The World's Most Famous Arena," provided an intimidating setting for a player who had been in college just days before. The pressure was immense, but Kreider's preparation at Boston College had helped build the mental toughness needed for such a moment.

His first NHL goal came at a crucial time, scoring the game-winner in Game 6 against the Ottawa Senators. The goal showcased his trademark speed as he burst past defenders before finishing with a precise shot. This moment announced his arrival as a legitimate

CHRIS KREIDER BIOGRAPHY

NHL player and helped the Rangers advance to the second round.

The Rangers' veteran players, particularly captain Ryan Callahan and alternate captain Brad Richards, took on mentorship roles with Kreider. They helped him navigate the intensified pressure of playoff hockey while adjusting to life in New York City. Their guidance proved invaluable during this challenging transition period.

Living arrangements during this period were temporary, with Kreider staying at a hotel near Madison Square Garden. This temporary situation reflected the uncertain nature of his position – he was neither a seasoned veteran nor a typical rookie, but rather a unique case of a player thrust directly into playoff competition.

CHRIS KREIDER BIOGRAPHY

The second round series against the Washington Capitals saw Kreider's confidence grow. He scored another game-winning goal in Game 1, becoming the first player in NHL history to score his first two career goals as game-winners in the playoffs. His speed and shooting ability were proving to be assets even against playoff-caliber defense.

Media attention intensified with each successful performance. New York's sports media is known for its scrutiny of athletes, but Kreider handled the pressure with remarkable poise. His education at Phillips Academy and Boston College had prepared him well for articulate interactions with the press.

The Rangers' coaching staff gradually increased Kreider's responsibilities as he demonstrated his ability to handle playoff pressure. His ice time grew, and he began seeing more important situations, including power play opportunities. The trust he earned during these playoffs would prove valuable for his future role with the team.

Team dynamics during the playoffs presented unique challenges. Unlike regular season rookies who have time to build relationships with teammates, Kreider had to integrate himself into an established group during their most important games of the year. His humble approach and willingness to learn helped ease this transition.

The physical demands of NHL playoff hockey were significantly different from college competition. The Rangers' strength and conditioning staff worked with Kreider to help him maintain his energy levels through the grueling playoff schedule. His exceptional conditioning from college proved beneficial during this intense period.

Tactical adjustments were necessary as Kreider learned the Rangers' systems on the fly. Coach Tortorella's aggressive forechecking style suited Kreider's speed and energy, but learning the defensive responsibilities required quick adaptation. Video sessions became crucial tools for accelerating his learning process.

The Eastern Conference Finals against the New Jersey Devils provided new challenges. The intensity of a conference finals series, combined with the rivalry between the teams, created an environment that tested Kreider's composure.

CHRIS KREIDER BIOGRAPHY

Despite the increased pressure, he continued to contribute effectively.

Throughout the playoff run, Kreider maintained contact with his Boston College coaches and teammates. Their support helped him maintain perspective during this whirlwind period. Coach Jerry York's guidance remained valuable as Kreider navigated the challenges of professional hockey.

The Rangers' playoff run eventually ended in the Conference Finals, but Kreider's performance had exceeded all expectations. His five goals and two assists in 18 playoff games represented remarkable production for a player making such an unusual transition to the NHL.

CHRIS KREIDER BIOGRAPHY

The experience gained during this playoff run proved invaluable for Kreider's development. He had faced the highest level of competition in the most pressure-filled situations possible, providing a foundation of experience that would benefit him throughout his career.

Madison Square Garden fans quickly embraced Kreider during these playoffs. His speed, scoring ability, and fearless play resonated with the New York crowd. The unique circumstances of his debut added to his appeal, creating a special connection with Rangers supporters.

The coaching staff's evaluation of Kreider's playoff performance helped shape plans for his future development. While he had shown remarkable ability, there were still aspects of his game that needed refinement for regular season

NHL success. This assessment would guide his development program during the following season.

Looking back on this debut period, the Rangers' decision to insert Kreider directly into playoff competition represented a significant risk that paid off. His success during these playoffs not only helped the team but also accelerated his development as a professional player.

Equipment managers and training staff remember the unique challenges of preparing Kreider for his debut. Everything from finding the right stick specifications to adjusting his skate sharpening preferences had to be determined quickly. His ability to adapt to new equipment while maintaining his performance level impressed the support staff.

The experience of playing alongside established NHL stars like Marian Gaborik and Henrik Lundqvist provided Kreider with examples of professional preparation and performance. Observing their routines and approaches to the game helped him understand what was required for long-term NHL success.

Financial aspects of his entry-level contract were structured to reflect his immediate jump to NHL competition. His contract began immediately upon signing, burning the first year during this playoff run. This decision reflected both the Rangers' commitment to him and their belief in his readiness for NHL competition.

As the playoffs concluded, Kreider had established himself as a legitimate NHL prospect with unlimited potential. His unique entry into professional hockey – jumping straight from college to the Stanley Cup playoffs – became part of Rangers lore and set the stage for his future success with the team.

The 2012 playoff debut represents a crucial chapter in Kreider's hockey journey, demonstrating his ability to perform under pressure and adapt to new challenges. This experience laid the groundwork for his development into one of the Rangers' core players and established his reputation as a clutch performer in important games.

CHAPTER 5: THE RANGERS DEBUT (2012)

After his remarkable playoff debut, Chris Kreider faced new challenges as he prepared for his first full NHL season with the New York Rangers. The fall of 2012, however, brought unexpected complications as the NHL entered a lockout. This forced delay would actually prove beneficial for Kreider's development, allowing him to ease into professional hockey through the American Hockey League (AHL).

During the lockout, Kreider joined the Rangers' AHL affiliate, the Connecticut Whale (now Hartford Wolf Pack). This experience provided valuable time to adjust to professional hockey's pace and physicality without the intense pressure of NHL competition. The AHL stint allowed him to refine his game and build confidence against high-level competition.

Working with the Whale's coaching staff, led by Ken Gernander, Kreider focused on developing the detailed aspects of professional hockey that weren't as emphasized in college. This included learning to manage the longer professional schedule, adapting to different defensive systems, and improving his play without the puck.

Life in Hartford presented a different challenge from New York City. The smaller market allowed Kreider to focus entirely on his development without the intense media scrutiny he had experienced during the playoffs. His colleagues in Hartford remember his dedication to improvement and willingness to learn from more experienced players.

When the NHL lockout ended in January 2013, Kreider returned to the Rangers with additional professional experience under his belt. However, the shortened NHL season presented its own challenges. The compressed schedule meant more games in fewer days, testing his physical conditioning and recovery abilities.

Head coach John Tortorella's demanding style presented both opportunities and challenges for the young forward. Tortorella's emphasis on two-way play and defensive responsibility pushed Kreider to develop aspects of his game that needed improvement. The coach's high expectations and direct communication style helped accelerate Kreider's understanding of NHL requirements.

The Rangers' veteran players continued their mentorship roles during this period. Players like Ryan Callahan and Derek Stepan helped Kreider navigate the adjustment to regular season NHL play. Their guidance extended beyond hockey, helping him adapt to life as a professional athlete in New York City.

Finding permanent housing in New York marked an important step in Kreider's transition to NHL life. He chose to live in Manhattan, embracing the city's energy while learning to manage the unique challenges of being a professional athlete in one of the world's largest media markets.

CHRIS KREIDER BIOGRAPHY

On-ice adjustments during this period focused on consistency and defensive awareness. While Kreider's speed and shooting ability remained exceptional, the coaching staff worked with him to develop a more complete game. This included improving his positioning in defensive zones and learning to use his size more effectively along the boards.

The pressure of playing in New York brought new challenges. Unlike his playoff debut, where adrenaline and novelty helped fuel his performance, the regular season required a different kind of mental toughness. Kreider worked with the team's mental skills coaches to develop routines that would help maintain his focus throughout the long season.

CHRIS KREIDER BIOGRAPHY

Madison Square Garden became more familiar territory as Kreider adjusted to his role. The historic arena's unique atmosphere and passionate fans created an environment that could be both inspiring and demanding. He learned to channel the energy of the Garden crowd while maintaining his composure in crucial moments.

Training routines evolved during this period as Kreider worked to maintain his exceptional speed while building the strength needed for NHL competition. The Rangers' strength and conditioning staff developed specialized programs that complemented his natural abilities while addressing areas that needed improvement.

CHRIS KREIDER BIOGRAPHY

Media responsibilities became a regular part of Kreider's professional life. His educational background served him well in handling interviews and public appearances. He developed a reputation among New York media for thoughtful responses and professional conduct, even during challenging times.

The team's travel schedule presented new challenges. Unlike college hockey, where most games were played regionally, NHL travel covered multiple time zones and climate changes. Kreider had to learn to manage his rest and recovery while maintaining peak performance despite frequent travel.

Special teams play became an increasing focus of Kreider's development. His speed made him a threat on the penalty kill, while his size and shooting ability made him valuable on the power play. The coaching staff worked to help him understand the nuances of these specialized situations.

Building chemistry with different linemates required adaptation and flexibility. Kreider's speed and skill set made him valuable in various line combinations, but each new combination required adjustments to timing and positioning. His ability to adapt to different playing styles proved valuable as the coaching staff experimented with various line combinations.

Off-ice preparation became increasingly sophisticated during this period. Kreider worked with the team's video coaches to study opponent tendencies and identify areas for improvement in his own game. This analytical approach helped him understand the strategic aspects of NHL competition.

Community involvement remained important as Kreider established himself in New York. He participated in various Rangers community initiatives, including youth hockey programs and hospital visits. These activities helped him connect with fans while maintaining perspective on his role as a professional athlete.

The physical toll of NHL competition required new approaches to recovery and maintenance. Kreider worked closely with the team's medical staff to develop routines that would help prevent injuries and maintain his performance level throughout the long season.

CHRIS KREIDER BIOGRAPHY

By the end of the 2012-13 season, he had experienced both the highs and lows of NHL competition. While his rookie season presented challenges, the foundation laid during this period would prove valuable for his future development. His unique path to the NHL – from college to playoffs to lockout to regular season – had provided experiences that would shape his approach to professional hockey.

Looking back, this initial full season with the Rangers represented a crucial period of adjustment and growth. The challenges faced and lessons learned helped transform Kreider from a promising prospect into a developing NHL professional. His ability to adapt and learn during this period set the stage for his continued evolution as a player.

CHRIS KREIDER BIOGRAPHY

The experience gained during this season helped shape Kreider's understanding of what it takes to succeed in the NHL. The combination of physical demands, mental challenges, and professional responsibilities provided valuable lessons that would influence his approach to the game throughout his career.

Today, this period is remembered as an important transitional phase in Kreider's development. While the statistics from this season might not reflect his full potential, the growth and learning that occurred during this time laid the groundwork for his future success with the Rangers.

The story of Kreider's first full NHL season demonstrates the challenges young players face when transitioning to professional hockey. His

CHRIS KREIDER BIOGRAPHY

experience serves as a valuable example for future prospects, illustrating the importance of patience, persistence, and adaptability in developing an NHL career.

CHAPTER 6: GROWING YEARS (2012-2017)

After his remarkable debut during the 2012 NHL playoffs, Chris Kreider's first few seasons with the New York Rangers represented a crucial developmental period both on and off the ice. As he transitioned from a promising prospect to an established NHL player, Kreider faced the challenges of finding consistency, dealing with injuries, and cementing his role within the team.

The shortened 2012-13 season, following the NHL lockout, provided Kreider with his first full taste of professional hockey's rigors. While his speed and scoring ability remained dynamic assets, the young forward quickly realized that sustained success in the NHL required a more complete, two-way game. Under the tutelage of head coach John Tortorella, Kreider focused on improving his defensive positioning, puck management, and overall consistency.

The coaching staff's emphasis on defensive responsibility was a significant adjustment for Kreider, who had often relied on his athleticism to dominate opponents in college and during his playoff debut. Adapting to Tortorella's demanding system required patience and a willingness to learn, as Kreider had to break certain habits and develop new instincts in his own zone.

Maintaining focus throughout the compressed 48-game schedule proved challenging. The physical and mental demands of the NHL were vastly different from the college game, and

CHRIS KREIDER BIOGRAPHY

Kreider occasionally struggled with the level of intensity required night after night. The support of veteran teammates, particularly captain Ryan Callahan and alternate captain Brad Richards, helped the young forward navigate these early professional challenges.

Off the ice, Kreider continued to adjust to life in New York City. Finding permanent housing, managing media responsibilities, and establishing a consistent routine became important aspects of his development. The Rangers organization provided resources to assist with this transition, recognizing the importance of a stable personal life for a player's on-ice performance.

Despite the ups and downs of his first full NHL season, Kreider's speed, size, and scoring ability continued to intrigue the Rangers' coaching staff. They saw the potential for him to develop into a valuable two-way forward, capable of contributing in all situations. The team's patience with his growth would prove crucial in the years to come.

The arrival of Alain Vigneault as head coach in 2013 brought a new philosophy and system to the Rangers. Vigneault's emphasis on puck possession and offensive creativity aligned well with Kreider's strengths, allowing him to showcase his dynamic abilities more consistently. Under the new coaching staff, the young forward began to find his rhythm and establish himself as a regular in the Rangers' lineup.

Injuries, however, became a challenge during this period. Kreider's physical style of play and relentless effort on the ice occasionally resulted in setbacks, including a hand injury that sidelined him for several weeks. Managing these setbacks and maintaining a positive attitude became an important part of his maturation process.

As the 2014-15 season progressed, Kreider began to demonstrate more consistency in his game. His scoring touch and two-way responsibilities were more in sync, and he developed into a reliable contributor on both special teams units. This evolution in his play earned him increased ice time and more prominent roles within the team's systems.

The Rangers' deep playoff runs during this era provided Kreider with additional opportunities to shine. His speed and scoring touch proved valuable in high-stakes situations, and he gained invaluable experience competing at the highest levels of the game. These pressure-filled postseason experiences helped reinforce the lessons he had learned during the regular season.

Off the ice, Kreider continued to be an active member of the New York community. He participated in various Rangers community initiatives, including hospital visits, youth hockey clinics, and charitable fundraising events. These activities not only endeared him to the team's fan base but also allowed him to maintain perspective on his role as a professional athlete.

CHRIS KREIDER BIOGRAPHY

By the 2016-17 season, Kreider had firmly established himself as a core part of the Rangers' lineup. His combination of size, speed, and scoring ability made him a versatile asset, capable of contributing in all situations. The coaching staff's trust in him was evident in the increased responsibilities he was given, including time on the top power play unit.

Navigating the challenges of a long NHL season became easier for Kreider as he gained more experience. His off-ice routines, including nutrition, recovery, and mental preparation, became more sophisticated, allowing him to maintain high levels of performance throughout the grueling schedule.

The 2016-17 campaign also marked a significant personal milestone for Kreider – the signing of a long-term contract extension with the Rangers. This deal not only provided him with financial security but also demonstrated the organization's belief in his long-term potential. It was a validation of the growth and development he had achieved during his first few seasons in the NHL.

As the 2012-2017 period came to a close, Kreider had evolved from a promising rookie to an integral part of the Rangers' score. His combination of size, speed, and skill made him a matchup problem for opposing teams, and his commitment to two-way play earned the respect of his coaches and teammates.

The "growing years" were not without their challenges, but Kreider's ability to adapt, learn, and persevere laid the foundation for his continued success with the Rangers. The lessons he learned during this formative period – about managing expectations, overcoming injuries, and developing a complete game – would prove invaluable as he entered the prime years of his NHL career.

The Rangers' organization and fanbase had witnessed Kreider's transformation from a college star to an established NHL player. His journey during these growing years served as a testament to the patience and support required to develop a talented prospect into a reliable, productive professional.

CHRIS KREIDER BIOGRAPHY

CHAPTER 7: LEADERSHIP EVOLUTION (2017-2020)

As Chris Kreider's career with the New York Rangers progressed, he continued to evolve not only as a player but also as a leader within the team. The years between 2017 and 2020 marked a significant transition, where Kreider's on-ice performance and off-ice impact became increasingly crucial to the Rangers' success.

By the 2017-18 season, Kreider had firmly established himself as a core member of the Rangers' roster. His consistent production, physical presence, and dedication to the team's success caught the attention of the coaching staff and his teammates. As veterans like Ryan McDonagh and Rick Nash departed, Kreider stepped up to fill the void, taking on a more prominent leadership role.

His natural charisma and respected work ethic made him a natural choice to guide the team's younger players. He became a vocal presence in the locker room, offering guidance and mentorship to newcomers. His willingness to lead by example, whether it was in grueling training sessions or intense game situations, earned him the admiration of his fellow Rangers.

Head coach David Quinn, who took over the team in 2018, recognized Kreider's invaluable qualities as a leader. "Chris has always been a leader, even before I arrived," Quinn remarked. "His dedication to the team and his ability to elevate the performance of those around him is truly remarkable. He's the kind of player every coach dreams of having in their lineup."

As his leadership role expanded, so too did his on-ice impact. The 2017-18 season saw him take a significant leap in his game, emerging as a true power forward. Utilizing his impressive combination of size, strength, and speed, Kreider became a dominant force in front of the net and along the boards.

Kreider's ability to win battles for pucks and create scoring opportunities for himself and his teammates became a crucial asset for the Rangers. He developed an uncanny knack for finding openings in the opposing defense, using his agility and quick hands to unleash precise shots or set up his linemates.

CHRIS KREIDER BIOGRAPHY

Opposing teams struggled to contain Kreider's relentless work ethic and physical presence. He became a nightmare for defenders, using his size and strength to shield the puck and create space for himself and his teammates. Kreider's willingness to drive to the net and engage in the dirty areas of the ice made him a constant threat, often drawing penalties and creating power-play opportunities for the Rangers.

"Chris has always had the physical tools, but what's really impressive is how he's honed his game to become a true power forward," said former Rangers captain Ryan McDonagh. "He's not just a pure scorer anymore; he's a complete player who can impact the game in so many different ways."

CHRIS KREIDER BIOGRAPHY

As the Rangers embarked on a rebuilding phase, Kreider's leadership qualities became even more valuable. With the influx of young talent, such as Kaapo Kakko, Alexis Lafrenière, and K'Andre Miller, Kreider took it upon himself to guide and mentor the next generation of Rangers.

Kreider's willingness to share his experiences and wisdom proved invaluable for the team's younger players. He would regularly pull them aside during practices, offering advice on everything from handling the pressure of the NHL to developing their individual skills. His ability to relate to the challenges faced by young players, having gone through a similar journey himself, made him a trusted confidant and role model.

CHRIS KREIDER BIOGRAPHY

"Chris has been an absolute godsend for us young guys," said Alexis Lafrenière, the Rangers' first overall pick in the 2020 NHL Draft. "He's always there to lend an ear, offer advice, and push us to be better. Having a veteran like him in our corner makes a huge difference in our development."

Kreider's mentorship extended beyond the ice as well. He often invited the younger players to his home, introducing them to his family and sharing insights into the importance of maintaining a healthy work-life balance. This personal touch helped the young Rangers feel valued and supported, fostering a strong team culture that would prove vital in the years to come.

His leadership and impact on the Rangers were not without their challenges. The 2017-18 and 2018-19 seasons saw Kreider battle through a series of injuries that threatened to derail his momentum.

In the 2017-18 campaign, a blood clot in his right arm sidelined Kreider for several months, forcing him to undergo a procedure to address the issue. The setback was a significant test of his mental and physical resilience, as he worked tirelessly with the team's medical staff to regain his strength and return to the ice.

The following season, Kreider faced another obstacle when he sustained a lower-body injury that kept him out of the lineup for several weeks. Despite the frustration and disappointment, Kreider remained focused on his recovery, using the time off to further refine his training regimen and work on aspects of his game that needed improvement.

"Chris is the kind of guy who never lets adversity get him down," said former Rangers goaltender Henrik Lundqvist. "He knows that setbacks are a part of the game, and he always comes back stronger than ever. That's the mark of a true leader – someone who can overcome obstacles and inspire the rest of the team."

Kreider's ability to bounce back from these challenges and maintain his high level of play was a testament to his dedication and commitment to the Rangers. His resilience and determination not only inspired his teammates but also solidified his reputation as one of the team's most valuable assets.

CHRIS KREIDER BIOGRAPHY

As the 2017-2020 period unfolded, Chris Kreider's evolution as a leader and power forward cemented his status as a cornerstone of the New York Rangers' roster. His impact on and off the ice continued to grow, making him an integral part of the team's present and future success.

CHAPTER 8: RECORD-BREAKING SEASONS (2021-2024)

The period between 2021 and 2024 marked the most remarkable phase of Chris Kreider's career with the New York Rangers, highlighted by unprecedented achievements, record-breaking performances, and a level of consistency that established him as one of the NHL's elite power forwards.

The 2021-22 season stands as a defining moment in Kreider's career, as he achieved what many considered impossible - scoring 50 goals in a single season. This milestone wasn't just a personal triumph; it represented the culmination of years of dedication, refinement of his skills, and an unwavering commitment to improving his game. The achievement was particularly notable as Kreider became only the fourth player in Rangers' history to reach the 50-goal mark, joining an elite group consisting of Vic Hadfield, Adam Graves, and Jaromir Jagr.

The journey to 50 goals began with a torrid start to the season, where Kreider demonstrated remarkable consistency in finding the back of the net. His ability to score in various situations - whether at even strength, on the power play, or in crucial moments - showcased his versatility as a goal scorer. A significant portion of his goals came from his exceptional net-front presence, where his hand-eye coordination, strength, and timing made him nearly impossible to defend against.

CHRIS KREIDER BIOGRAPHY

The historic 50th goal came in a game against the Carolina Hurricanes at Madison Square Garden, a moment that brought the home crowd to their feet and highlighted Kreider's importance to the franchise. The goal itself was emblematic of his playing style - a deflection from the front of the net, displaying his trademark ability to find space in dangerous areas and redirect pucks past opposing goaltenders.

Rangers head coach Gerard Gallant praised Kreider's achievement, noting, "What Chris has accomplished this season is extraordinary. It's not just about the number of goals, but how he's scored them and the impact they've had on our team's success. He's been a dominant force every night, and this milestone is a testament to his hard work and dedication."

The 2021-22 season wasn't just about individual achievements for Kreider. His scoring prowess played a crucial role in the Rangers' successful campaign, helping the team secure a playoff position and make a deep run in the postseason. His leadership qualities continued to shine as he guided younger players through the pressure-packed atmosphere of playoff hockey.

Beyond the 50-goal milestone, Kreider's evolution as a complete player became increasingly evident. His defensive game showed marked improvement, and his ability to contribute in all situations made him an indispensable part of the Rangers' lineup. The coaching staff relied on him in crucial moments, whether protecting a lead late in games or trying to generate offense when trailing.

One of the most impressive aspects of Kreider's record-breaking season was his dominance on the power play. His ability to position himself effectively in front of the net, combined with his quick hands and hockey intelligence, made him one of the league's most dangerous power-play threats. He set a new franchise record for power-play goals in a season, surpassing Jaromir Jagr's previous mark.

The following seasons saw Kreider continue to build on his success, though matching the 50-goal mark proved challenging - as it would for any player. However, his consistent production and leadership remained vital to the Rangers' success. His ability to maintain a high level of play while dealing with the increased attention from opposing teams demonstrated his growth as a player.

The 2022-23 season, while not matching the goal-scoring heights of the previous year, showcased Kreider's ability to impact games in multiple ways. His focus on becoming a more complete player led to improved defensive statistics and an increased role in mentoring younger teammates. He continued to be a force on the power play, using his experience and skill to create scoring opportunities for himself and his linemates.

The evolution of his game during these seasons was particularly evident in his ability to adapt to different linemates and situations. Whether playing alongside skilled playmakers or more physical forwards, he maintained his effectiveness and found ways to contribute to the team's success. His versatility became one of his greatest assets, allowing the coaching staff to use him in various roles depending on the team's needs.

Off the ice, his leadership qualities continued to shine. His role as a veteran presence in the locker room became even more crucial as the Rangers integrated new players into their lineup. Young players consistently praised his willingness to share advice and provide guidance, both during practices and games.

The 2023-24 season saw Kreider reach more milestones, including surpassing 300 career goals with the Rangers, further cementing his place in franchise history. His consistency and durability remained remarkable, as he continued to play a physical, demanding style while maintaining his effectiveness.

His impact on the Rangers' success during these seasons extended beyond statistics. His presence on the ice often created opportunities for teammates, as opposing teams were forced to account for his combination of size, speed, and skill. This attention frequently opened up space for other players, leading to increased offensive production throughout the lineup.

The veteran forward's influence on special teams remained significant, particularly on the power play. His ability to screen goaltenders, redirect shots, and battle for position in front of the net made the Rangers' power play one of the most feared in the NHL. Coaches and teammates alike praised his willingness to absorb the physical punishment that comes with playing this style, noting his toughness and determination as key factors in the team's success.

During this period, Kreider's preparation and attention to detail served as an example for younger players. His commitment to maintaining peak physical condition and constantly working to improve his skills demonstrated the level of dedication required to succeed in the NHL. The Rangers' training staff often highlighted his work ethic and professional approach as model behavior for developing players.

The impact of his record-breaking seasons extended beyond individual achievements. His success helped establish a winning culture within the Rangers organization, setting high standards for performance and professional conduct. His ability to maintain excellence while handling increased expectations showed his mental toughness and maturity as a player.

As these seasons progressed, Kreider's importance to the Rangers franchise became increasingly evident. His consistency, leadership, and ability to perform in crucial moments made him an invaluable asset to the team. The organization's decision to commit to him long-term proved prescient, as his contributions both on and off the ice helped shape the team's identity and success.

The period from 2021 to 2024 will be remembered as the time when Chris Kreider truly established himself as one of the Rangers' all-time greats. His record-breaking achievements, combined with his leadership and consistent performance, created a legacy that will influence the franchise for years to come. Young players coming into the organization now had a clear example of what it meant to be a professional, both in terms of on-ice performance and off-ice conduct.

These seasons also saw Kreider further strengthen his connection with Rangers fans. His work ethic, commitment to the team, and memorable performances made him a beloved figure at Madison Square Garden. The relationship between Kreider and the Rangers faithful grew stronger with each passing season, as fans appreciated not just his goal-scoring prowess but also his dedication to the team and the city.

CHRIS KREIDER BIOGRAPHY

Looking back at this period, it's clear that Kreider's success was no accident. It was the result of years of development, hard work, and a constant drive to improve. His record-breaking seasons served as a validation of his approach to the game and his importance to the Rangers organization. As the team continued to evolve and compete for championships, Kreider's contributions during these years stood as a testament to his impact on the franchise and his place in Rangers history.

The legacy of these record-breaking seasons extends beyond individual statistics. Kreider's performances helped establish a standard of excellence within the organization, influencing how future generations of Rangers players would approach their careers. His success served as proof that dedication, perseverance, and a willingness to continually evolve as a player could lead to extraordinary achievements.

CHAPTER 9: THE HEART OF BROADWAY

Chris Kreider's impact on the New York Rangers extends far beyond his statistical achievements and on-ice performances. His connection to Madison Square Garden and New York City has made him an integral part of the Rangers' identity and a beloved figure in the heart of Broadway.

Madison Square Garden, often referred to as "The World's Most Famous Arena," has been the stage for many of Kreider's most memorable moments. His relationship with the historic venue began during his playoff debut in 2012 and has only grown stronger over the years. The Garden faithful have witnessed his evolution from a promising rookie to a franchise cornerstone, creating a special bond between player and fan base that exemplifies the unique relationship between Rangers players and their supporters.

Throughout his tenure with the Rangers, Kreider has demonstrated a deep appreciation for the history and tradition associated with playing at Madison Square Garden. In numerous interviews, he has spoken about the privilege of wearing the Rangers jersey and the responsibility that comes with representing the organization in such an iconic venue. "There's something special about stepping onto the ice at MSG," Kreider once remarked. "The energy, the history, the fans – it's unlike anything else in hockey."

CHRIS KREIDER BIOGRAPHY

The connection between Kreider and Rangers fans has grown organically over the years, built on a foundation of mutual respect and appreciation. Fans have consistently praised his work ethic, determination, and commitment to the team. His style of play – physical, aggressive, and relentless – resonates particularly well with the Garden crowd, who have long appreciated players willing to sacrifice their bodies for the team's success.

His popularity among fans is evident in the number of jerseys bearing his name and number that can be seen throughout Madison Square Garden on game nights. His autograph sessions and fan meet-and-greets consistently draw large crowds, with supporters of all ages eager to interact with a player who has become synonymous with Rangers hockey in the modern era.

Beyond his on-ice contributions, he has embraced his role as a Rangers ambassador in the New York community. His involvement in various charitable initiatives and community outreach programs has demonstrated his commitment to making a positive impact beyond hockey. The Garden of Dreams Foundation, the Rangers' primary charitable organization, has particularly benefited from Kreider's active participation and support.

One of the most significant aspects of Kreider's community involvement has been his work with youth hockey programs in the New York metropolitan area. He regularly participates in clinics and training sessions, sharing his knowledge and experience with young players aspiring to follow in his footsteps. His ability to connect with young athletes and provide meaningful guidance has helped strengthen the Rangers' presence in local hockey communities.

His impact on the Rangers' culture cannot be overstated. As one of the longest-tenured players on the team, he has played a crucial role in maintaining the organization's traditions while helping to establish new standards for excellence. His professionalism, dedication to improvement, and leadership qualities have influenced countless teammates who have passed through the Rangers' locker room.

The veteran forward's understanding of what it means to be a Ranger has made him an invaluable resource for new players joining the organization. Whether they're highly-touted prospects or established veterans, newcomers to the team often cite Kreider as a key figure in helping them adjust to playing in New York and understanding the expectations that come with wearing the Rangers jersey.

Madison Square Garden has witnessed numerous memorable moments in Kreider's career, from his playoff debut goal to his 50th goal of the 2021-22 season. Each milestone has helped strengthen his legacy as a Rangers icon and deepen his connection with the arena that has become his hockey home. The Garden's unique atmosphere and passionate fanbase have provided the perfect backdrop for Kreider's career achievements.

As a cultural ambassador for the Rangers, Kreider has shown a deep appreciation for the team's history and traditions. He often speaks about the legendary players who have worn the Rangers jersey before him and the responsibility of upholding the organization's standards. His knowledge of Rangers history and respect for those who came before him has earned him admiration from alumni and fans alike.

The relationship between him and the New York media has also been notably positive throughout his career. His thoughtful responses to questions, willingness to be accessible, and ability to handle both success and adversity with grace have made him a respected figure among journalists covering the team. This professional approach has helped him effectively communicate the team's message to fans and maintain a positive public image for the organization.

In the fast-paced world of New York sports, where athletes can quickly fall in and out of favor with fans and media, Kreider's consistent presence has provided stability and reliability for the Rangers organization. His ability to maintain high standards of performance and professionalism while dealing with the pressures of playing in New York has set an example for his teammates.

The impact of his presence at Madison Square Garden extends to the business side of the organization as well. His popularity has contributed to merchandise sales, ticket demand, and the overall brand strength of the Rangers. Marketing executives within the organization have praised his authenticity and relatability, noting how these qualities have helped strengthen the connection between the team and its fanbase.

His role as a Rangers culture ambassador has been particularly evident in his interactions with fans during community events. Whether visiting hospitals, participating in charity functions, or attending fan appreciation events, he has consistently demonstrated genuine care and interest in connecting with supporters. His ability to make meaningful connections with fans of all ages has helped strengthen the bond between the team and its community.

The veteran forward's influence on Rangers culture can also be seen in how he carries himself away from the rink. His professional approach to training, preparation, and recovery has set a standard for younger players to follow. Teammates often speak about learning from his example, whether it's his dedication to maintaining peak physical condition or his attention to detail in game preparation.

Throughout his time with the Rangers, Kreider has embraced the unique challenges and opportunities that come with playing in New York City. He has managed to maintain a balance between being accessible to fans and media while preserving the focus and dedication needed to perform at a high level. This ability to navigate the demands of playing in a major market has made him an invaluable asset to the organization.

CHRIS KREIDER BIOGRAPHY

As his career has progressed, his status as a Rangers icon has only grown stronger. His longevity with the team, combined with his significant contributions both on and off the ice, has earned him a special place in Rangers history. Future generations of players will likely look to his example as they seek to understand what it means to be successful in New York.

The heart of Broadway has seen many great players wear the Rangers jersey, but few have embraced the role as completely as Chris Kreider. His connection to Madison Square Garden, the fans, and the city of New York has created a legacy that extends far beyond his statistical achievements. As he continues to add to his Rangers story, the bond between player and city remains as strong as ever, serving as a testament to the impact one player can have on a franchise and its community.

Through his years with the Rangers, Kreider has demonstrated that success in New York requires more than just on-ice performance. It demands an understanding of the city's hockey culture, a commitment to the community, and an appreciation for the privilege of playing at Madison Square Garden. His ability to excel in all these areas has made him not just a successful player, but a true embodiment of what it means to be a New York Ranger.

CHAPTER 10: PERSONAL LIFE AND VALUES

Beyond the bright lights of Madison Square Garden and the intense world of professional hockey, Chris Kreider has cultivated a rich personal life grounded in strong values, family bonds, and diverse interests that have helped shape him both as a player and as a person.

Family has always been at the core of Kreider's life journey. Growing up in Boxford, Massachusetts, he was raised in an environment that emphasized education, hard work, and personal growth. His parents, David and Kathy Kreider, played instrumental roles in developing his character and work ethic from an early age. Their support and guidance helped lay the foundation for his future success, both on and off the ice.

Kreider's commitment to education, a value instilled by his family, has remained constant throughout his career. Despite the demands of professional hockey, he completed his degree in Communications from Boston College, attending classes during off-seasons. This achievement reflects his belief in the importance of personal development beyond athletics and his understanding that a hockey career, while demanding, should not preclude other forms of growth and learning.

In 2019, Kreider married Stephanie Rupert, whom he met during their time at Boston College. Their relationship has provided a strong foundation of support as he navigates the demands of professional hockey. Stephanie, herself an accomplished former soccer player, understands the unique challenges of elite athletics and has been a crucial partner in Kreider's journey. The couple maintains a private but balanced life in New York, where they've established strong connections within the community.

Away from hockey, Kreider has developed a variety of interests that help him maintain perspective and balance in his life. An avid reader, he often speaks about his love for literature and history, interests that were cultivated during his years at Phillips Academy Andover and Boston College. His intellectual curiosity extends to learning languages – he is conversant in Russian and Spanish, skills he has occasionally used to help international teammates adjust to life with the Rangers.

Kreider's commitment to fitness and nutrition has become legendary within the Rangers organization. His training regimen extends beyond standard hockey preparation, incorporating innovative approaches to strength, speed, and recovery. He has worked closely with the Rangers' strength and conditioning staff to develop a comprehensive program that addresses the specific demands of his power forward playing style while maintaining long-term health and durability.

His dedication to physical preparation includes a meticulous approach to nutrition. Kreider has become known for his detailed understanding of sports nutrition and its impact on performance.

CHRIS KREIDER BIOGRAPHY

He often shares his knowledge with younger teammates, helping them understand the importance of proper fueling for elite athletic performance. His own diet is carefully planned to support his training and recovery needs, demonstrating the level of commitment required to maintain peak performance at the NHL level.

Charitable work has become an increasingly important part of Kreider's life off the ice. He has been particularly active in supporting youth hockey initiatives and educational programs in the New York area. Through the Rangers' community outreach programs, he has worked with various organizations that provide opportunities for underprivileged children to experience hockey and receive academic support.

His involvement with the Garden of Dreams Foundation has been particularly meaningful. The foundation, which works with children facing obstacles, has given Kreider numerous opportunities to make a direct impact in young people's lives. Whether through hospital visits, hockey clinics, or mentoring sessions, he has shown a genuine commitment to using his platform as a professional athlete to benefit others.

His approach to training has evolved significantly throughout his career. Working with various specialists, he has developed a comprehensive understanding of athletic performance that goes beyond traditional hockey training. His regimen includes elements of power skating, plyometrics, and specialized strength training designed to maintain the explosive power that has become a hallmark of his game.

Recovery and injury prevention have become increasingly important aspects of his training philosophy. Kreider has embraced modern approaches to recovery, including advanced nutrition strategies, sleep optimization, and various therapeutic modalities. His attention to these details has contributed to his ability to maintain a high level of performance throughout the grinding NHL season.

Mental preparation is another crucial component of Kreider's approach to professional hockey. He has worked with sports psychologists and mental performance coaches to develop techniques for maintaining focus and managing the pressures of playing in New York. These skills have proven valuable not only in his own performance but also in his role as a mentor to younger players.

Throughout his career, Kreider has maintained strong connections to his roots in Massachusetts hockey. He regularly returns to his hometown during the offseason, working with local youth programs and maintaining relationships with coaches and mentors who influenced his early development. These connections help keep him grounded and remind him of the journey that brought him to the NHL.

His personal values are reflected in his approach to leadership within the Rangers organization. Kreider emphasizes the importance of accountability, hard work, and team success over individual accolades. These principles, learned from his family and early mentors, have shaped his development as a leader and influenced the Rangers' team culture.

Time management has become a crucial skill for Kreider as he balances the demands of professional hockey with his personal life and various interests. He has developed effective strategies for maintaining this balance, ensuring that he can fulfill his responsibilities as a professional athlete while nurturing important relationships and pursuing personal growth opportunities.

The importance of giving back to the community has been a constant theme in Kreider's life. He regularly participates in Rangers alumni events, working to maintain the connection between past and present players while helping to raise funds for various charitable causes. His involvement in these activities reflects his understanding of the responsibility that comes with being a professional athlete in New York.

Kreider's personal life also includes a strong appreciation for the arts and culture that New York City offers. He and his wife enjoy exploring the city's museums, theaters, and restaurants during the season, taking advantage of the unique opportunities that come with living in one of the world's great cultural capitals.

His commitment to continuous learning extends to his hockey career, where he regularly studies film and analyzes different aspects of the game. This intellectual approach to hockey has helped him adapt and evolve as a player, contributing to his longevity and success in the NHL.

CHRIS KREIDER BIOGRAPHY

The values that guide Kreider's personal life – commitment to education, family, fitness, and community service – have helped shape him into more than just a successful hockey player. They have created a foundation for a well-rounded life that extends beyond the rink and sets an example for others in the organization.

As his career has progressed, Kreider has maintained a remarkable balance between the intense demands of professional hockey and the development of a fulfilling personal life. His success in managing these different aspects of his life serves as a model for younger players and demonstrates that athletic excellence need not come at the expense of personal growth and community engagement.

CHAPTER 11: PLAYING STYLE ANALYSIS

Chris Kreider's evolution into one of the NHL's most distinctive power forwards represents a fascinating study in player development and specialized skill refinement. His unique combination of size, speed, and skill has made him a formidable presence on the ice and a challenging matchup for opponents throughout his career.

At 6'3" and 220 pounds, Kreider possesses exceptional physical attributes that form the foundation of his playing style. However, it's his ability to combine this imposing frame with remarkable speed that truly sets him apart. Former Rangers coach David Quinn once noted,

CHRIS KREIDER BIOGRAPHY

"What makes Chris unique is that you rarely find someone his size who can skate like he does. It's a combination that creates constant problems for opposing teams."

Speed has always been a defining characteristic of Kreider's game. His acceleration and top-end speed are particularly noteworthy for a player of his size. This exceptional skating ability was developed during his early years and refined through countless hours of power skating training. Rangers skating coach Barbara Underhill, who has worked extensively with Kreider, has praised his dedication to improving his skating mechanics and maintaining his explosive speed.

The technical aspects of Kreider's skating style are worth analyzing in detail. He generates tremendous power from his stride, utilizing his strong lower body to create explosive acceleration. His edge work, particularly in tight spaces, allows him to maintain control while operating at high speeds. This combination of power and precision in his skating has become increasingly rare in the modern NHL, especially for a player of his size.

One of the most notable aspects of Kreider's game is his effectiveness in front of the net. Over the years, he has developed into one of the NHL's premier net-front presences, particularly on the power play. His ability to screen goaltenders, deflect shots, and battle for position in this high-traffic area has become legendary within the league. Former teammate Henrik Lundqvist often praised Kreider's skill in this area, noting how difficult it was for goaltenders to track pucks with him establishing position in front.

The development of his hand-eye coordination, especially for deflections and tip-ins, has been remarkable. This skill didn't come naturally but was instead the result of countless hours of practice. He regularly stays after team practices to work on tip drills, focusing on subtle adjustments in stick positioning and timing that can make the difference between a deflected goal and a missed opportunity.

His power forward style is also characterized by his physical play along the boards and in open ice. While not known as a frequent fighter, he uses his size effectively to win puck battles and create space for teammates. His ability to protect the puck while maintaining speed makes him particularly effective in transition play, often allowing him to turn defensive situations into offensive opportunities.

The evolution of his shot has been another crucial component of his playing style. While Kreider has always possessed a powerful shot, his release has become quicker and more accurate over the years. He's developed particular effectiveness with his one-timer, especially from the slot area, adding another dangerous element to his offensive arsenal.

An often-overlooked aspect of Kreider's game is his defensive responsibility. As his career has progressed, he's become increasingly reliable in his own zone. His speed allows him to backcheck effectively, while his strength helps him clear the defensive zone and transition to offense. This two-way ability has made him valuable in all situations, earning the trust of multiple coaching staffs.

Training and preparation play a crucial role in maintaining Kreider's unique playing style. His off-season regimen focuses on maintaining explosive power while ensuring his body can withstand the physical demands of his game. This includes a combination of traditional strength training, plyometrics, and specialized skating work designed to maintain his speed advantage.

The mental aspects of Kreider's game have evolved significantly throughout his career. His ability to read plays and anticipate developments on the ice has improved markedly, allowing him to better utilize his physical gifts. This hockey

IQ, combined with his natural attributes, has made him an increasingly complete player.

His effectiveness on the power play deserves special attention. His ability to establish position in front of the net, read the play, and make split-second adjustments has made him one of the league's most dangerous power-play threats. The Rangers have built much of their power-play strategy around his net-front presence, using his skills to create scoring opportunities both directly and indirectly.

The evolution of his puck handling skills has added another dimension to his game. While not typically known for fancy stickhandling, Kreider has developed efficient puck control that allows him to maintain possession while using his speed and size to create advantages. This improvement has made him more effective in one-on-one situations and in maintaining offensive zone possession.

One of the most impressive aspects of Kreider's playing style is his durability. Despite playing a physically demanding game and constantly battling in high-traffic areas, he has maintained remarkable consistency in his availability. This durability is a testament to his conditioning program and attention to recovery protocols.

Leadership on the ice has become an increasingly important part of Kreider's playing style. He leads by example with his work ethic and compete level, setting a standard for intensity and preparation that influences his teammates. His vocal presence on the bench and during games helps maintain team focus and energy.

Analyzing Kreider's success in various game situations reveals the versatility of his playing style. He's effective at even strength, excels on the power play, and can be trusted in defensive situations. This adaptability makes him valuable in all phases of the game and allows coaches to deploy him in various tactical situations.

The consistency of Kreider's playing style has been remarkable. While he has added elements to his game over the years, the core attributes – speed, power, and net-front presence – have remained constants. This consistency, combined with strategic improvements, has allowed him to maintain effectiveness even as the league has evolved.

CHRIS KREIDER BIOGRAPHY

Video analysis of Kreider's play reveals subtle details that contribute to his success. His positioning away from the puck, the timing of his net-front moves, and his ability to find soft spots in defensive coverage all demonstrate a sophisticated understanding of the game that complements his physical tools.

The impact of his playing style extends beyond his personal statistics. His presence on the ice often creates opportunities for teammates, whether through drawing defensive attention, creating screens, or opening up space with his speed. This ability to make those around him more effective has become an important part of his value to the team.

CHRIS KREIDER BIOGRAPHY

Looking ahead, Kreider's playing style appears well-suited for longevity in the NHL. His combination of size, speed, and skill, along with his attention to conditioning and recovery, suggests he can maintain effectiveness even as he ages. The technical foundation of his game, particularly his skating and net-front skills, should continue to serve him well.

The influence of Kreider's playing style on younger players in the Rangers organization is evident. Many prospects study his approach to net-front play and power skating, recognizing the value of developing these specific skills. His success has provided a template for how to effectively combine physical tools with technical skills in the modern NHL.

EPILOGUE

As Chris Kreider's story continues to unfold on Madison Square Garden ice, his journey from a promising Massachusetts prospect to one of the New York Rangers' most impactful players offers both reflection and anticipation. Looking back at his career while considering the path forward provides valuable insights into his legacy and future aspirations.

When reflecting on his NHL journey, Kreider's evolution stands as a testament to dedication and continuous improvement. From his dramatic playoff debut in 2012 to becoming one of the franchise's most prolific goal scorers, his development has been remarkable. The milestone of scoring 50 goals in the 2021-22 season marked a pinnacle achievement, placing him in elite company among Rangers legends.

Throughout his career, Kreider has demonstrated an exceptional ability to adapt and grow. His early years showcased raw speed and potential, but it was his commitment to developing specific skills – particularly his net-front presence and deflection abilities – that transformed him into a complete power forward. This evolution didn't happen by chance; it was the result of countless hours of specialized training and a relentless drive to improve.

The relationship between Kreider and the Rangers organization has been mutually beneficial. The team provided him with the patience and support needed to develop, while he has rewarded their faith with consistency, leadership, and production. His long-term commitment to the organization, evidenced by his contract extension in 2020, speaks to the strong bond between player and team.

The impact of Kreider's presence extends far beyond statistics. His role in mentoring younger players, maintaining team culture, and representing the organization in the community has helped shape the modern identity of the Rangers. Former teammates and coaches consistently praise his influence on team dynamics and his commitment to fostering a professional environment.

Looking ahead, Kreider's objectives remain aligned with team success. The pursuit of a Stanley Cup championship continues to drive him, understanding that his prime years coincide with the Rangers' competitive window. His dedication to maintaining peak physical condition and continuing to refine his game demonstrates his commitment to this goal.

Personal development remains a priority for Kreider. His intellectual curiosity and desire to expand his knowledge, both within hockey and beyond, suggest he will continue to grow as a player and leader. The combination of his experience and ongoing dedication to improvement positions him to remain effective as the game continues to evolve.

Kreider's place in Rangers history is already secure, but his legacy continues to grow. His achievements – including franchise records for power-play goals and his 50-goal season – have earned him a permanent place among the team's greatest players. However, it's his impact on team culture and his role in bridging different eras of Rangers hockey that may prove most significant.

The connection Kreider has forged with Rangers fans is particularly noteworthy. His authentic approach to the game, commitment to the organization, and consistent performance have earned him devoted support from the Madison Square Garden faithful. This relationship exemplifies the special bond that can develop between a player and the New York fanbase.

Beyond individual accomplishments, Kreider's influence on the next generation of Rangers players may be his most lasting contribution. His example of professionalism, work ethic, and dedication provides a blueprint for young players entering the organization. The standards he has helped establish will influence the team's culture long after his playing days conclude.

As Kreider continues his career, several factors suggest sustained success. His playing style, built on a foundation of exceptional skating and net-front skills, appears well-suited for longevity. The attention he pays to conditioning and recovery, combined with his tactical intelligence, should allow him to adapt as necessary while maintaining effectiveness.

The evolution of the NHL presents both challenges and opportunities. The game's increasing speed and emphasis on skill align well with Kreider's abilities, while his size and power provide advantages that remain valuable in the modern game. His ability to combine these elements makes him uniquely suited for success in today's NHL.

The relationship between Kreider and the Rangers organization seems poised for continued growth. His role as a leader and mentor becomes increasingly valuable as the team integrates young talent, while his on-ice contributions remain crucial to the team's success. The mutual commitment between player and organization provides a stable foundation for future achievements.

Beyond hockey, Kreider's journey continues to encompass personal development and community involvement. His interests in education, languages, and culture suggest a rich life beyond the rink, while his charitable work demonstrates a commitment to giving back to the community that has embraced him.

The balance Kreider has achieved between professional excellence and personal growth offers valuable lessons for athletes at all levels. His example shows that pursuing athletic success need not come at the expense of broader development, and that maintaining diverse interests can contribute to sustained performance.

As Chris Kreider's story continues to unfold, his journey represents more than just athletic achievement. It stands as a testament to the power of dedication, the importance of continuous growth, and the special relationship that can develop between a player and a storied franchise. While many chapters remain to be written, his impact on the New York Rangers and the sport of hockey is already significant and enduring.

The future holds both promise and challenge, but Kreider's approach to both success and adversity throughout his career suggests he will continue to meet whatever comes with characteristic determination and professionalism. As he adds to his legacy with each passing season, his story remains an inspiring example of what can be achieved through talent, dedication, and unwavering commitment to excellence.

Made in the USA
Monee, IL
02 December 2024

71993736R10085